RABBIT LANGUAL

or, "Are you going to eat that?"

A humorous guide to communicating with your pet rabbit.

SECOND EDITION

by Carolyn "R" Crampton

HOWELL
PARK
PRESS

Thanks to Mary Melquist and Alane Bowling for editorial advice. Thanks to the
House Rabbit Society for the idea of adopting Lassie from the pound.

ISBN 978-0-9793088-0-2 *Rabbit Language or Are you going to eat that? Second Edition* published by Howell Park Press, San
Francisco, CA, www.howellparkpress.com. Text and graphics ©2007 Carolyn R Crampton. All rights reserved.

For my teachers and models:
Lassie, Lucy, Ike, Malcolm Little, Slushie and Chester.

IT IS a mistake to think of rabbits as lacking a language just because we don't take the time to learn it. Domesticated animals have lost the civilization they had in the wild. But they have instincts and whatever life lessons are learned in the short time they spend with their mother.

RABBITS are clever about manipulating humans and can seem stubborn about learning how to live in our homes.

It helps to see things through rabbit eyes: a wire is a root that needs trimming; a piece of furniture is a tree; a household is a rabbit warren with strict hierarchy and rules.

For twenty years, my rabbits trained me to understand their bunny body language. Here is what I have learned.

Behavior

LYING with one ear raised.

What it means

Someone may be opening the refrigerator.

What you should do

Forget feeding yourself until you give your sweetie-pie fresh dandelion greens.

Behavior

RINDING teeth while petting the head.

Commonly thought to mean

Pleasure, like cats' purring.

What it may mean

Among rabbits, the dominant One allows grooming by lesser beings if they perform the sacred rite of head petting.
Perhaps grinding also lingers from when Momma Rabbit licked baby's head to encourage drinking milk.

What you should do

Murmur sweet nothings to your sweet bunny.

NOTE: Loud grinding or grinding without petting may mean your rabbit is in pain and needs to go to the vet asap.

Behavior

RUBBING chin on things, such as houseplants, priceless armoires, Italian leather shoes.

What it means

A great misconception: It does *not* mean *marking territory*. It is a rabbit custom, like saying grace before a meal. In short, "One day I will eat you."

What you should do

Give your bunny more sticks and branches, keep your stuff off the floor, and kiss the antiques goodbye.

Behavior

BALANCED on hind legs, little front feet in the air.

What it means

Classic begging pose. Also means "Let's see if I can grab that food out of your hand."

What you should do

Lower your hand to make it a fair fight.

Behavior

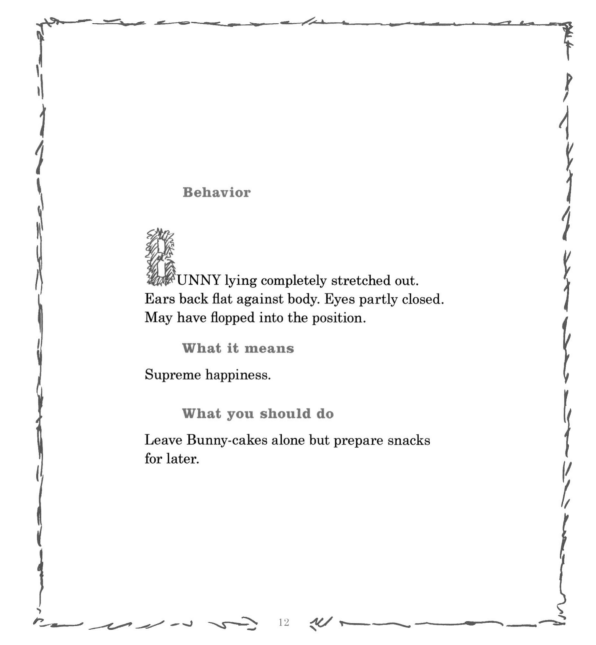

BUNNY lying completely stretched out.
Ears back flat against body. Eyes partly closed.
May have flopped into the position.

What it means

Supreme happiness.

What you should do

Leave Bunny-cakes alone but prepare snacks
for later.

Behavior

RABBIT sitting on your shoes as you are trying to lace them.

What it means

Rabbits have a long history of foot worship. The bigger the feet, the bigger the attraction. In the case of a rival male (such as a boyfriend or a husband), the bigger the feet, the bigger the threat.

Anything which adorns feet is a big turn-on. As everyone knows, feet just smell good.

What you should do

Clearly it is more important for you to stay home than apply shoes and socks.

If you are the presumed rival, do not stand around and flaunt your assets—sit on the floor and be friendly.

Behavior

NECK stretched out. Eyes widened. Ears way back. Somehow the effect is of a much younger, thinner animal. This behavior often performed when you are on the way out of the house.

What it means

"I am starving and alone. I am your helpless baby bunny. Feed me. Don't leave me alone."

What you should do

Take off your coat and stay home.

Behavior

MALE RABBIT: Hopping in circles around you with tail up, grunting or humming.

Variations:

Hopping in or out of your legs, possibly carrying a checkbook end, stick or some other highly-desirable item, biting your feet, trying to get you to hop over him. Spraying.

What it means

Courting Behavior: "Those are big sexy feet you have. I will have sex with them."

What you should do

Quickly sit on your feet.

Behavior needing research

SMILING.

How can you tell?

I do not know how, but you *can* tell. A rabbit
smile is unmistakable. It's in the eyes.

Behavior

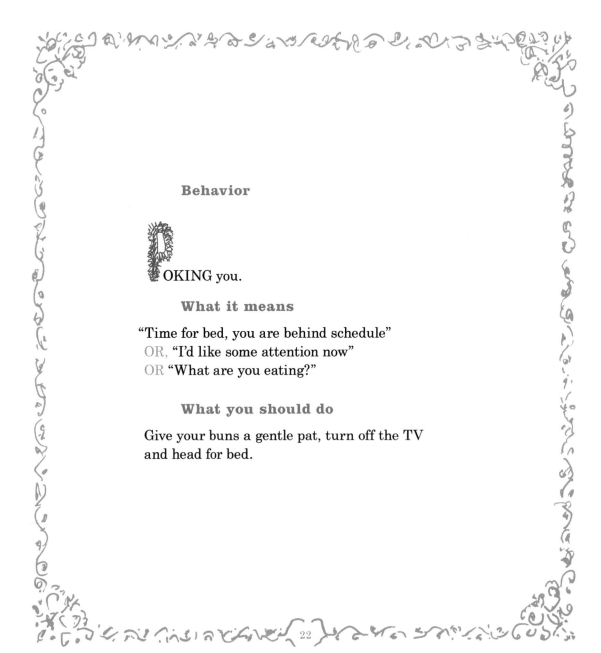

POKING you.

What it means

"Time for bed, you are behind schedule"
OR, "I'd like some attention now"
OR "What are you eating?"

What you should do

Give your buns a gentle pat, turn off the TV
and head for bed.

Behavior

JUMPING up in the air and kicking one's heels.

What it means

Happy to see you.

FEMALE RABBIT:
I'm ready to have sex now.

What you should do

Be very glad you have such a happy bunny. Treat yourself to chocolate ice cream.

Behavior

EARS tilted forward. Eyes widened. Neck stretched out, nose twitching. Low crouch, legs back in the last time zone.

What it means

Caution. Curiosity mixed with fear. Exploring a new area, a strange animal.

What you should do

Bunnies need to investigate the world. Make sure your bunny is safe and be sure there are no scary predators (such as large dogs) around.

Behavior

UPRIGHT. Half raised on back legs, ready for flight and stomping. Eyes wild and open. Thumping.

What it means

"Danger." "Get underground." "The phone is ringing." "How did this plant [i.e., chair] change location?"

Stomping also means sexual excitement, happiness, or maybe you dropped a sock on the floor.

What you should do

Get up and run over—before the whole neighborhood wakes up—to soothe your bunny.

Behavior

SLEEPING in different locations at regular times of the day.

What it means

Ancient rabbit behavior of guard duty. Rabbits guard the entrances to the den. OR, if there is spot of sun shining on the floor, chances are your rabbit is lying in it. OR, may also involve watching veggies grow.

What you should do

Arrange furniture so there are lots of interesting tunnels to run through and places to catch some rays.

Behavior

EXCESSIVE and prolonged licking.

What it means

You are petting bunny's back and thereby activating the licking instinct. OR, you have recently stopped your petting.

What you should do

Repeated strokes on the top of the head is the preferred method. Skritchy-skratchy on the lower back with your nails is also acceptable.

Behavior

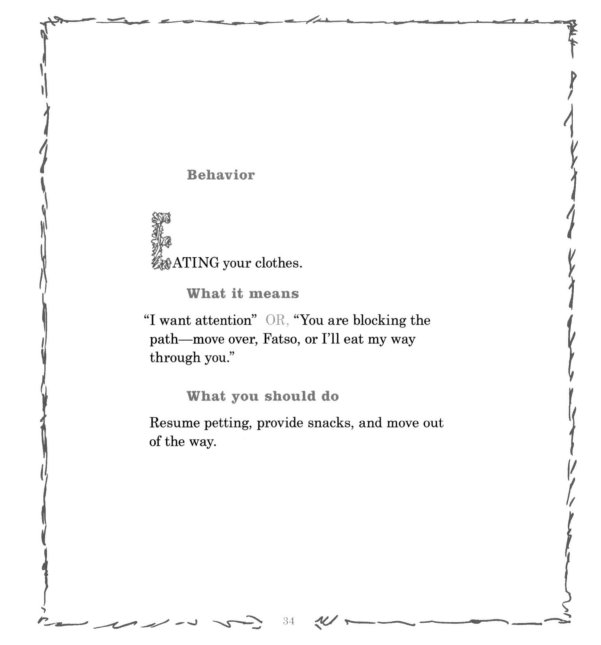

EATING your clothes.

What it means

"I want attention" OR, "You are blocking the path—move over, Fatso, or I'll eat my way through you."

What you should do

Resume petting, provide snacks, and move out of the way.

Behavior

THROWING things around. Excessively loud eating. Rhythmic paper tearing.

Commonly thought to mean

"Feed me." OR, "I am angry."
OR, "Wake up and feed me."

Actually is

Ancient rabbit musical composition often performed at length on Saturday mornings while you are trying to sleep in.

Fun experiment

Don't set the alarm clock. Bunnykins knows when you are supposed to get up and will kindly wake you, unless you did something horrible like smearing laxative on a paw the night before.

Behavior

INCESSANTLY jumping on your head and digging in your hair while you are trying to sleep, no matter how many times you say "Get off the [expletive deleted] bed you [expletive deleted] animal!"

What it means

Snookems is afraid there is something wrong with you. OR, you have fresh veggies hidden under your pillow.

What you should do

Stop trying to sleep, get up and play with your rabbit.

Considerations:

Are you sleeping at the wrong time? Are you sleeping with someone else? Your rabbit may be trying to protect you or may be jealous.

Behavior

FEMALE RABBIT: Ripping out her own fur and collecting it in her mouth. Later burying it in your bedsheets when you are not looking. Running around the house with small stuffed animals or socks in her mouth.

What it means

"This is where I am having my babies."

What you should do

Move out of your bed and sleep on the floor where you will be available for late night petting.

Behavior

BITING things (like wires) that bunny knows are off limits. OR, crazed biting.

What it means

Honey-pie is angry. Rabbits have a real temper. They do not like being treated like pets.

What you should do

Hold some paper or a stick in front of Honey-pie's mouth so that it can be ripped to shreds. (Keep fingers well away from teeth.)

Try a loud sniff to show your anger—some rabbits sniff when angry.

Behavior

GNAWING on remote control. OR, repeatedly knocking over your choice of beverage.

What it means

Your bunny is not trying to switch to the Nature Channel. Bunny craves dietary variety.

What you should do

Although plastic is made from oil, and oil is organic, do everything in your power to keep plastic and other household items from being eaten.

Fermented grain or fruit may be encountered in the wild, but do not feed your bunny beer or wine. No one likes a rabbit with a drinking problem.

Behavior

ITING and growling.

What it means

"I had my pile of hay all carefully arranged, and now look at it!" OR: "Who are **you** to come into **my** territory?"

You are trying to clean Snuggles's area. Rabbits hate change. This includes nail clipping, brushing and medicating. OR, you may be trying to put the rabbit into a cage.

What you should do

Wear gloves and get another person to help you. OR, wrap Snuggles up in a towel like a burrito while you work on a limb. If you are lucky, you may get "I'm kinda digging these shorter nails."

Behavior

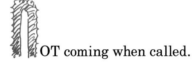OT coming when called.

What it means

"Name one good reason why I should come over there."

What you should do

Tap the floor while shaking a fragrant, fresh green leaf. Lie on your back and wait for your bunny's natural curiosity. A nice treat in your hand is always welcome.

Related annoying behavior

Lying exactly one arm's length away from you. (Don't you just hate it when bunnies do this?)

THREE related behaviors, often observed in older and wiser rabbits, sometimes in combination:

Shaking the trailing foot while hopping away

What it means

"Ick…I don't want that after all."

Shaking head or ear once or twice

What it means

"This is too much! What, are you crazy?"

Shoulder shiver

What it means

"I'm not eating that", OR "No Way"
OR "Whatever, freak!"

Behavior

EAD buried in the belly.

What it means

Digging out tasty morsels to eat. Yes, rabbits digest their food twice. Some pellets come out as dry round rabbit raisins (found scattered on your carpet or stuck to your shoe) and other pellets are smelly, steamy, and apparently very delicious.

What you should do

You might want to reconsider all that kiss kiss.

WHATEVER you do, think carefully before getting a rabbit for a pet. Rabbits will wreck your home, destroy your relationship with your boyfriend and cause your friends to ridicule you behind your back. Your home will smell like a barn and there will always be rabbit raisins on the carpet. Shedding seasons are blizzards of fur.

Oh, you may become popular as that wacky party guest with the hilarious rabbit stories—such as the time you spent thousands on bunny's dental surgery or weekly acupuncture treatments. But you can never, ever, have friends over for supper.

If you must have a rabbit for a pet, adopt an older one from the pound or a rabbit rescue group in your area. (No one wants to live with a rabbit going through puberty, not even you.) If living with a small horse in the apartment appeals to you, then you may be rabbit material. Order a bale of hay and "Tally Ho."

~ the end ~

For tips on caring for your rabbit or information about *Rabbit Language*, visit www.cramptonarts.com/rabbits.

For up-to-date medical information, visit the House Rabbit Society (www.rabbit.org).

CPSIA information can be obtained
at www.ICGtesting.com
Printed in the USA
LVIC06n2037050115
421583LV00008B/171